# Dancing on the X

*poems by*

## Todd Williams

*Finishing Line Press*
Georgetown, Kentucky

# *Dancing on the* X

Copyright © 2025 by Todd Williams
ISBN 979-8-89990-169-0  First Edition
All rights reserved under International and Pan-American Copyright Conventions. No part of this book may be reproduced in any manner whatsoever without written permission from the publisher, except in the case of brief quotations embodied in critical articles and reviews.

Publisher: Leah Huete de Maines
Editor: Christen Kincaid
Cover Art: Heidi Williams
Author Photo: Todd Williams
Cover Design: Elizabeth Maines McCleavy

Order online: www.finishinglinepress.com
also available on amazon.com

Author inquiries and mail orders:
Finishing Line Press
PO Box 1626
Georgetown, Kentucky 40324
USA

# Contents

America, Maybe ................................................................................. 1

**When We Danced**
Dancing on the X ........................................................................... 19
The Cosmos ................................................................................... 21
Portrait with Pinwheel ................................................................... 22
Afternoon Delight .......................................................................... 23
Sunday Mornings with the Crusher .............................................. 24
Out of Bounds Call (Deadwood Junior High vs. Crazy Horse) ... 25
The Beatles vs. Styx, 1981 .............................................................. 26
Meet Me Tonight beneath the Carnival Lights So We Can Say
    Goodbye to Summer ................................................................. 28
Where the Streets Have No Name ................................................ 29
Confessions of a Killer Poet .......................................................... 30
73 Seconds ..................................................................................... 31
When We Dissolve (Saying Goodbye at Rapid City Regional
    Airport for the Last Time, Thanksgiving 1991) ...................... 32
Rudderless ...................................................................................... 33
Mixtape .......................................................................................... 34
They Dance (Sunday Night at Nelly's) ......................................... 35

**Love in a Time of Caldera**
Advanced Dungeons & Dragons & Deliverables ........................ 39
Accidental Kiss .............................................................................. 40
Snow Day with Sophia .................................................................. 41
Star Wars and Everything After .................................................... 42
Pluto Falls ...................................................................................... 43
nine-eleven .................................................................................... 44
Lamentations ................................................................................. 45
My Pandemic Face ........................................................................ 46
The New Normal ........................................................................... 47
The Closest I'll Ever Come to Knowing (What It's Like to Drive
    while Black) ............................................................................... 48
Get Small ....................................................................................... 49
An Open Letter to Old Ben Kenobi .............................................. 50
Mitch McConnell Stares Out at the Sea ....................................... 52
Flight 370 ....................................................................................... 53
See-Unsee-Sonder ......................................................................... 54

**A Mouthful of Moon**
  Funeral Songs .................................................................................. 57
  The Dead Don't Remember .............................................................. 59
  The Glacier Reminds Me of What It's Like to Grow Old ............... 60
  Smoke ................................................................................................ 61
  Of Love and Rust .............................................................................. 63
  Forgive Me Lord for I Know Not What I Do ................................. 64
  In the Morning, I Narrowly Escape an Aneurysm while Putting
     On My Socks for the Day ............................................................. 66
  The Shape of Morning ..................................................................... 67
  Father 1.0 ........................................................................................... 68
  I Wear My Dead Father's Socks ....................................................... 69
  Watching ESPN after 2 a.m. ............................................................. 70
  My Brilliant Tattoo ........................................................................... 71
  Armageddon Didn't Come Today ................................................... 72
  Menomonie, Wis. .............................................................................. 74
  After the New Moon ........................................................................ 76

**Acknowledgments** ............................................................................. 77

*For my bean, my wife, my everything (and fellow X'er) Heidi*

**America, maybe**

we keep missing the point
and should heed the warnings
mounting outside our door,
in junk mail folders,
across TV scrolls
morning, noon, and night.
Maybe the flashing light
that signals from the dashboard,
that hangs over perilous intersections,
that calls from outside your room at night
is a sign from the other side
something may be askew.
Beware! Beware! Beware!
the consequence of climate change,
low testosterone, high cholesterol,
and using the same password
over and over again.
Beware the cures for painful disease
and their long list of side effects
that make it seem as if suffering
might be sublime compared
to enduring that trail of fears.
Beware the lure of too much salt,
too little kale, and making your money
work hard so you can be happy once
you retire at the spry age of 83.
Beware the fascists, and anti-fascists, too,
and anyone who's refused to wash their hands
after having used the restroom, public or otherwise.

**America, maybe**

we've forgotten how great
a gift you've been, your history
celebrated in films, books, and songs
for so long your meaning begins to fade
even as the volume rises.
Sometimes someone forgets
you were an idea first,
not a flag,
not a bumper sticker,
nor a theory of conspiracy
wrapped in some riddle that can only be solved
by those who watch one news show over another.

**America, maybe**

I love you more in absentia,
sweet smell of forests burning,
mournful hum of tires on asphalt,
sharp breath of morning pinching
my skin on a crisp September day.
The longer I stay away,
the more you remain the same,
a story told and retold until
it's little more than white noise.
When I close my eyes and dream
of what you mean to me,
it's always 1999, and tomorrow
couldn't be further away.

**America, maybe**

you were born in redaction,
a sentence handed down decade
after decade, defeat after defeat,
every third word stricken
from your permanent record,
whole paragraphs rent in rendition.
It isn't that we didn't learn our history;
it's that we couldn't learn yours,
be it boarding school burials
or massacres in Tulsa and L.A.,
Nixon's plans learned by LBJ,
or that long line of excuses
on why we bombed Iraq,
from WMDs to the need for a peace
kept under lock and key.
Brick by opaque brick you built
fables faithful to God and home,
courage and progress, freedom
and fairness and prosperity
and democracy, dozens upon dozens
of words repeated like rosary prayers,
their blood-stained husks carpeting
the ground we walk upon.

**America, maybe**

we're not getting enough sleep,
Deep State fears and endless streaming
pushing us into the red, dead tired
as we stumble toward an oblivion
predicted long before Orwell.
The promise of automation and AI
was supposed to lead to lives of leisure
not seen since Fantasy Island left the air,
but your tired masses are only growing
more tired and more massive.
Willingly we submit to the miasma
of us versus them, common sense,
and dense arguments about what
some men centuries ago would think
about the internet, or gender reassignment,
or whether sugar should be classified as a drug.
These are the things that keep us awake
at night, waves of emotion leaving little room
for insight or contemplation, the night light
of worry staring us down from across the room.

**America, maybe**

you were never more than
a promise in the year of election,
an endless selection of facts
and slander disguised as opinion,
your truth lying in the words
of those who sell sunshine
to the homeless and fear
to the distracted,
damned,
and delivered.

**America, maybe**

you're the garden of Eden,
Beelzebub riches tempting
the faithful and wicked alike.
Maybe you're the Tower of Babel
stretching toward the heavens,
an endless stream of information
and entertainment eradicating
any space for reflection.
Or maybe you are Gethsemane,
shadows falling fast around
as enemies surround the garden,
guardians slumbering at your feet.

### America, maybe

we should think hard about our history
and try not relive it, myriad myths
and realities wrapped like onion layers
around a seed no one's ever seen,
nor maybe ever should.
It seems we're always becoming
what we've already been, scanning
the horizon like it's a QR code
or signpost on the road to Nirvana,
coffee-thick clouds obscuring
the shimmering black road before us.

**America, maybe**

enough will never be enough,
this hunger to glean meaning
from five second snippets and sound
bites, tweets, memes, and reels
consuming purple mountains
and fruited plains from the inside out.
We learn to speak in pictures
and howl in live-time video.
Shout, sing, scream, or dance
in delight, try as we might,
we can never go home,
we can never go home,
we can never go home
to your sepia-rich utopia
conjured and then cast as memory.

**America, maybe**

Phoenix has grown too hot
and Duluth too cold, the highways
that once brought us together crumbling,
your rust-riveted bridges collapsing
into swift waters that yearn for the sea.
The straight lines that brought us here
are no longer true, Rand McNally
having long ago abandoned Atlas
and the weight of the world.

**America, maybe**

you are more than the sum
of your obsessions, baseball, apple pie,
and Mom melding into a stew
of automatic weapons, proper pronouns,
angry politics, felines in cyberspace,
nuclear weapons, solar power,
lottery jackpots in the billions,
expensive cars, cheap gasoline,
and memes in a single screen.
Tax refunds, sexual tension,
and family time thirst for attention,
as do spell-checking phones,
deals on the down low, and credit
cards that delay payments due.
America, your love is boundless
and super-sized, calories dripping
from colorful cardboard boxes,
hearts growing bit by bit
until they're about to burst
in a hail of bullets and sweet kisses,
the believers and ambivalent
coming together in their mourning.

**America, maybe**

it's time to accept some difficult truths:

Oswald acted alone

temperatures are rising

and we spend way too much
time on our mobile phones.

**America, maybe**

if we'd paid more attention
in civics class, or at church,
or at something other than
whatever sedative is buzzing
in our ears as we pass neighbors
and friends while offering little
but scant nods, only then we might find
space for more of your dreams,
more music, more color,
more brotherhood, more compassion,
more riches than we could ever imagine,
and maybe room to become something more.

**America, maybe**

your certitude is blight.
We the people wander through days
with only Google maps to guide us,
but the man on the other side of the line
demands we make life decisions in less time
than it takes to perform long division.
Assigned a number, then two, five,
nineteen, and ad infinitum, our paths
are preordained by unseen algorithm,
slight breezes begetting hurricane winds
that press us to one side of the fishbowl
or the other.

**America, maybe**

two-hundred-fifty years
is a very long time—
maybe not for Europe,
nor for the Milky Way,
nor for the universe as a whole,
but really a remarkable stretch
for a democracy to thrive.
Sometimes, the patient knows not
the gravity of their condition,
picking at scabs and bedsores
while they wither, the scent
of death on the wind.

**America, maybe**

you never know
what you have
until it's gone.

*When We Danced*

**Dancing on the X**

We hatched no plans
from the backs of sedans
nor beneath stuttering streetlights,
secret winks and Pig Latin veiling
a lack of intent and promise that one day
we would have to rule the world.
Not in the way our parents did,
choked in sulphury clouds of cigarette smoke
and the wintry tint of rum and Coca-Cola,
but with a wisdom gleaned firmly
from latchkey summers and school days
that were more survived than celebrated.
We found our truths bound
to the backs of Beetle Bailey
and his ilk, a collection
of X-ray specs, sea monkeys,
dribble glasses, and strong defense
by plastic green army men.
Born before or around the bicentennial,
we found no faith in freedoms
our parents revered, no love
of the exceptional, no strength
in American dreams deferred
for those unlike ourselves.
Instead, we rose in our disinterest
in everything but baseball cards
and beer can collections,
sarcasm, red stripe Nikes,
and long autumn nights spent
sipping bad beer while bathed
in the rich perfume of woodsmoke.
If the world were our oyster,
we were its grit, losing ourselves
in seas of baggy jeans, patchouli oil,
fat-free sweets, and confidence
that the X on our treasure maps
marked a spot safe from all
the pitfalls our parents endured.

And still, we ended up here,
fathers and mothers and brothers
swept away in an ocean of fear
of how technology defines our time,
every update delivered,
every clock aligned,
every moment refined
by algorithm sans happenstance.
We become like Wile E. Coyote
when he at last caught the Road Runner,
turned to the screen, and then asked,
*Now what do I do?*

## The Cosmos

Little America, Devil's Tower,
and a thousand miles of two-way highway
filled windshields painted by insect remains
in the summer of our only family vacation,
days stretching forever as we squirmed
across sun-stained leather seats
and listened to the radio fade in and out
through a wind-bent antenna.
Tourist traps were our only redemption,
humbled outposts along forgotten trails
between Reno and Rushmore,
hand-drawn signs signaling
our sleepy but eager eyes.
**STOP** the car and
**SEE** the **SPECTACULAR,**
**WORLD'S BIGGEST,**
**MOST POPULAR** and
**RECENTLY FEATURED** in
*Ripley's Believe It or Not.*
Best of them all stood tall in the shadow
of the Presidents themselves, skewed
shacks and wonders of science
called The Cosmos.
For just a few dollars, we four could stand
in collective awe of nature's laws
reversed as balls rolled up hills.
Try as we might, we were unable to fall,
so much mystery married to the deception.

## Portrait with Pinwheel

Thick mittens could hardly hold
its frozen wind-whipped whirl,
a blur of reds, greens, and blues
that colored those duotone days in Duluth.
Four years old and fearless I blew
with all my breath through cracked lips,
trying so hard to accelerate the twirl,
tinny wings rattling as if they could escape
their ninety-nine-cent frame.

I begged for it to turn faster and faster,
but then you took my hand and spoke
to me of love, bubble gum, and the moon.
You offered such deliberate words
to help me comprehend how much
you hoped for nothing more
than to slow the spin a little and freeze
this moment with a photograph,
the place where we first began to fade.

**Afternoon Delight**

That one summer you were Mother's favorite song,
hanging in the air like a light June breeze,
a saccharine salute to A.M. radio
and all things John Denver.
We sang your lyric from the top of our lungs,
a suggestive swirl too worldly
for our grade school ken to comprehend.
Now when I hear you on oldies shows
or by the spin of the digital DJ,
no embarrassment rises when words return
and rise from my lips, muscle memory recalling
a family vacation in the back seat of a '73 Datsun,
the smell of leaded gasoline and cigarette smoke
choking childish voices in a cloud of nostalgia.

### Sunday Mornings with the Crusher

In the glory of weekend mornings he ruled,
a barrel-chested man prancing from rope to rope
as hopes rose and swooned with each
exaggerated

          fall,
every bloodied face,
and all those SLLLINGSHHHHOT, canvas-rattling,
mercy-denying, pile-driving clashes enacted
upon and by the magnificent crew
of the original All-Star Wrestling.

Like the Claw, Flying Dutchmen, and Mad Dog Vachon,
he grew larger than life in a living room transformed
into an arcane theater of violence and gymnastics
as comic book dialogue spilled from our console TV.
Barefoot and alone we'd scream,
wince, and bellow with delight
as they enacted their revenge upon each other,
our excitement too real to care where
the action followed a script, or not.
Later, when the adults weren't looking, we'd practice
our flying leaps onto the feathery surface of our beds
and imagined one day we, too, would rule the ring.

Oh, how wonderful it was to have such villains.
Oh, how we wept when we found it just a ruse.

## Out of Bounds Call (Deadwood Junior High vs. Crazy Horse)

*White ball* the referee called
and with his words delivered
a sentence to every player
who ran the court that day
in January of my eighth-grade year.

We wore orange and black;
they wore red and white.
But as the tall man in polyester slacks
and vertical striped shirt blew his whistle,
he handed me the ball and colored my world forever.

## The Beatles vs. Styx, 1981

After the second bus broke down
just a few miles from home,
coaches packed the first so tight
it was certain to start a row;
we just didn't know how
it would happen.

Some hundred teens
too weary to safely sail
their emotional seas pushed,
pulled, sweated, and stared out
cracked windows at the highway
ahead, wishing to be anywhere else
than so close to Wyoming.
We laughed too loud and tried
to drown out the sound of our own
anxiety, our own restlessness,
our own insecurities that exploded
in a series of hair pulls, yowls,
and general ill ease among the restless mob.
Arguments sprang up about some
of the finer points of junior high life:

*Does Sea Breeze prevent acne?*
*How can you sneak "chew" into school?*
*Do you think she's gone all the way?*

The sway of conversation grew
to a low roar until the smallest seed
swept all the others beneath its bead.
He said *Paradise Theater* was the best
album he'd heard in his 13 years
and that Styx reigned supreme.
I gasped, guffawed, and huffed
that ignorance was no excuse
for someone with half a brain.

*The Beatles, now there was a band.*

And that was my glaring mistake,
believing that those too young
to legally drive, to buy beer,
to understand the nuance
of *The Tonight Show with Johnny Carson*
could ever understand
there were things in this world
our parents were right about.
But with a loud cry and showman's
flair dressed in disdain,
he rained down upon my countenance
a storm of shame I can still feel
in my gut some 45 years later.
To top it off, he took a poll
of what side my fellow passengers fell,
and when the counting was done,
Styx notched seventy-six, the Beatles had one.

**Meet Me Tonight beneath the Carnival Lights
So We Can Say Goodbye to Summer**

Lift a last hurrah and let it be lost
amid the shrieks and screams
untethered by manic machines
and the prospect of another season passed.
Walk among the sun-baked barkers
and long-haired keepers who cast eager eyes
on cowboys, college kids, and teens
too trusting in Midway illusion,
one curated by a pony-tailed man with tattoos
who offers little more than raised eyebrows
and long strings of paper ticket rewards.
The rich mystery of his sleeve, dipped
in warm colors, comes alive in the crystalline glow
of a thousand mini-turbo bulbs, stark white suns
casting shadows on the faces of neighbors.
Let's wait together in line for the vertigo
thrills on The Bullet or Tilt-O-Whirl.
Saturday night is fading,
and the sweet half-moon with it.
Soon, all that will remain will be
the fleeting pungence of cotton candy
and diesel fuel, our ears overwhelmed
by bells, shrieks, and heavy metal
as we bid farewell to these strangers,
our familiar escorts to summer's end.

**Where the Streets Have No Name**

Sitting before the altar of the old Bonneville Brougham,
I lean back and close my eyes, bathed in the plastic cherry
bouquet of a freshly opened Joshua Tree cassette case.
It's Tuesday, and church is just seconds away.
From steep silence, the moment grows
across a horizon drawn first in a low hum, then rising
all around, from a crawl to a gallop to a sprint.
I am left breathless in this micro-flash of eternity.

Years from now in the post-Napster apocalypse
that is the recording biz, there will be no number of words
able to describe to my children the wonder
of the many things that brought the music to us—
the joy in stripping cellophane from tightly wrapped packages,
fold-out lyrics and posters taped to our bedroom walls,
and the long hope for rare bonus tracks hidden from our view.
They will only ask, *What did you use your phones for?*

## Confessions of a Killer Poet

I am the butcherer of birds,
a slayer of petulant flies,
an assassin of ants.
I've murdered mice,
put down pets, then killed
weeds and flowers alike
in the name of beauty and love.
A man with grand ambition,
I've laid waste to gray paper
nests of angry hornets and wasps,
crushed the fleeting dreams of gnats,
and drowned a thousand spiders
in the silvery circle of my tub.
Some call me kind and Christian,
but as a boy against unforgiving rocks
I splayed the intestines of a speckled trout,
its unblinking eyes wide with terror.
On Highway 212 in the fall,
I've left behind the bodies of beasts
of all sizes; mosquitoes, skunks,
deer, and even sheep have failed
to escape my grim reap.

My friend Paul swears that nature
must be feared and respected,
that she is forever out to get us,
so it's our right to be the first to strike.
But my pacifist grandfather took
great measures to preserve all life,
eschewing swatters and rolled-up
newspapers, choosing instead a glass
and yellow legal notepad to usher
uninvited guests back into the wild.

I pause to ponder, then listen
for the thump of a pigeon's body
across the broad undercarriage of my car,
hoping against hope it was only a rock
as I scan rear view mirrors to find
a supernova of white feathers
rising from the black asphalt behind.

## 73 Seconds

The steely ship climbed,
detonated, then disappeared
in countless pixels of smoke,
a fiery white cumulus cloud
raining down confusion
on my classmates and me
as we watched on an old TV
in Allen Hall dorm.
We stood wide-eyed in disbelief,
not really sure what we were seeing
as debris splintered blue skies
and the broadcast fell silent.

How strange the pain that washed
across us, an ocean of cathode rays
pressing across the breadth
of our chests, the congregation
of men barely more than boys
still as winter's breath.

We watched.

We waited.

And no one spoke as we stepped
outside into the bright chill of January.

Nearly four decades on, that sting
still smolders, meaning more molded
by my fellow witnesses than the stories
that followed about safety, O-rings,
and what it was like to be there.
Today we face the disasters alone,
bent in reverence to tiny screens
and streams of bad news that never relent,
the test patterns of our youth no longer playing
well into the morning and ringing in our ears
as we rolled over and drifted back to sleep.

**When We Dissolve (Saying Goodbye at Rapid City Regional Airport for the Last Time, Thanksgiving 1991)**

The turbo-prop taxied, turned,
then rose into cloudless skies,
a tiny blinking light growing smaller
until you were as a star extinguished.
Fallow fields painted by a whisper
of snow stretched toward horizons
half waiting for dusk, sunset spilling
its rust across the prairie and runway below.
I stared with watery eyes into an appreciating abyss
as photocell lights flickered to life,
the glass canvas of Gate Six clean and clear
as it cast nothing back but my own reflection.

**Rudderless**

Evan Dando sings my soul,
slack jawed and inert
on this November day, 1993.
Wrapped in the warm essence
of patchouli oil and dirty socks,
the faint promise of sleep
seems just one weekend away
when he and Juliana come to me,
tripping over the space heater
and sending a box full of cassettes
and half-stale Nutter Butter cookies
crashing to the shag carpet below.
Their tiny fragments fall between
furry brown worms of fabric
where they will soon be forgotten,
fugitives from a hastening hunger for more.
If you need me, this is where I hang.

**Mixtape**

You are a mixtape in a basement
box, buried beneath rusting paper clips
and long-since aborted journals.
The hiss of time's passing nips
at waxy ears, cresting waves slapping
against cobwebs that drape
this muted room like an April snow,
all cold and warm at the same time.
Together we list as I ease back
into the soft arms of a frayed recliner,
its once-rich brown having faded
to gray in the corners where dust-drawn
fingers of sunlight have failed to reach.
Wrapped in blankets of memory, I hum.
Words have no place in this twilight,
clicks and pops of magnetic resonance
disrupting the flow of uneven ripples
as they stretch across the stillness.
The symphony swells and heart races,
a siren song to the unreachable.
It is not you I miss; it's me.

## They Dance (Sunday Night at Nelly's)

On Sundays, they dance
when others seek sleep,
spend time with families
or make plans for the week.

Dealers and doormen
and waiters just through
with weekend shifts
and the money they blew
for a quick hit of crank
and red beer with olives,
seven hands of blackjack,
some smokes, and the call of
desperate days.

Up the street and down
the stairs, Nelly's by seven,
they'll drink away cares
of classes and weekdays
and jobs with no future.
A step to the left,
a step to the right,
they purge their guilt
and throw their hands in the air,
and they dance.

They dance to remember,
they dance to forget,
they dance to be brave
and feel no regret.
They dance in tight quarters
and on through the night
with Cowboy Curtis,
Dick Burns, and the like.

They dance with their friends,
and they dance much too close,
they dance with a frenzy
as sweat stains their clothes,

this song of their youth
rising a chorus,
in their darkness a fire
that shines right before us.

A step to the left,
a step to the right,
they down one last shot.
As the clock strikes twelve,
Kenan flips on the lights,
and they dance.

*Love in a Time of Caldera*

## Advanced Dungeons & Dragons & Deliverables

In collared shirt and khaki pants,
I gird myself for labyrinths of treachery
and villainy not known since eight-tracks
and Trapper Keepers filled locker shelves.

With the dim light of an iPhone 5 leading
the way through days abloom with Zoom calls
and cubicle walls, I struggle to map progress
across graph paper and overdue performance reviews.

What I wouldn't do to find my way back
to that 12-year-old self, no knowledge nor fear
of strange beasts lurking around blind corners
or conference rooms, adventure's call ringing loudly.

To succeed at business without even trying,
all I'd need is my strong sense of justice
and a two-handed sword aflame with truth,
chaotic evil bowing to 18+ strength at every turn.

Synergy and teamwork would grow despite differences,
elves, dwarves, halflings, and humans together
enduring dire campaigns that'd loom like a lycanthrope
beneath a blood red moon, Lean Six Sigma our common foe.

And after battle, we'd gather to drink our frothy grog
from Starbucks, waving wands and magic markers while taking
comfort in games played without winners, the treasure
no small measure of X's marking our corporate calendars.

**Accidental Kiss**

daylight lingers
in cool streams
of the A/C,
your bare shoulder
rising and falling
with each breath

these sacred seconds
seem far too brief,
hanging in the air
like dandelion dust
at the lips of a child

you exhale and send
an accidental kiss
toward my side of the bed,
today's blessings
drifting toward the infinite

**Snow Day with Sophia**

Arms thrown high over her head
as if this were a holdup, the girl
sleeps while infant dreams seep
from a mouth half ajar.
The old house groans
under two feet of snow,
a surprise spring storm
effacing electricity and all paths
of escape in its wake.

I pull her tiny body to my chest;
we breathe as one in the stillness.

Years ago, mother held me close
too long, too, tears streaming
from her eyes as I said goodbye
and drove off for college,
reminding that I'd be back
by Thanksgiving.

But lying here wrapped
in the warmth of a home
trapped in strong weather,
I come to understand at last
my careless disregard
and what it's like to swim in love,
to feel the world's pull,
and what it is to become.

**Star Wars and Everything After**

My son will never see Star Wars,
or at least the movie I saw
in that Wisconsin summer of '77,
the taste of popcorn and RC Cola
still lingering after all these years.
Drawn to the cool darkness
of a theater long since shuttered,
I can still feel the orchestra erupt
in a rush of Dolby Surround Sound.
It shakes my boyish chest as sights
and sounds of fantastical worlds
are born in flickering light.
From old wooden chairs we peer,
my wide-eyed companions and I,
at heroes and villains and then
nothing in between how things were
and how they would forever be.
But like my mother before me
with the King and his swiveled hips
hidden from horizontal holds,
or grandma's delight when the girl
stepped from sepia hues
into the Emerald City,
my son will hold fast to worlds
I can never understand except
for the fascination as he pulls back
the thick curtains of childhood,
someday sharing tales of a time
as magical, or more, than mine.

**Pluto Falls**

Maybe it began with Milli Vanilli,
or perhaps Barry Bonds;
it could have even been the war in Iraq,
but too many things that once were true
are no longer.

Never mind the tooth fairy, Santa Claus,
or even the laws of gravity reversed in the Cosmos;
I fear the things that weren't meant to deceive.

Not seeing the Great Wall from outer space;
the same swirl of toilets south of the equator;
no onions at the doors of plague-fearing farmers.

Carrots couldn't sharpen my sight,
handling toads offered no warts,
and no length of time need pass
between eating and hitting the pool.

Sometimes, I feel a fool for once believing
that bats were blind,
cracked knuckles would curl,
and that Everest towered supreme.

But the biggest tragedy
came with the fall of Pluto,
diminished in rank from childhood
songs and maps of our solar system
to a mere dwarf in the realm of planets.

It did not shrink.
It did not reverse orbit.
It did not change in any way,
and yet the powers that be
somehow stole its honor.

I sit and stare up at cloudless skies
and wonder when, not why,
we'll someday turn them white.

**nine-eleven**

Our ghosts live in those seven seconds,
a severing silence stretched from after the first jet
and then the next punched holes in Manhattan's skyline,
fiery orange blossom swallowing blue skies
and sunshine in clouds of jet fuel and fear.

Anchors fell quiet,
politicians paused,
preachers pursed their lips;
teachers shushed,
children hushed,
even the crickets ceased to chirp
while we held our tongues.

And when the world began to spin
again, we were flung from its axis
into a void so vast it stole our breath.

## Lamentations

Old man rambling on about everything
that's wrong with this world leaves
his laundry list of laments unmoored
at the door of your thought.
There's so much he dislikes.
**QR codes for menus, Guinness in a can,**
the world of **self-service lanes** and **automated tips,**
he lets rip his litany of complaint.
Then there's **Thursday night games**
and endless waves of **traffic** that grow longer each season.
**Network TV, cable TV,** and **streaming services**
spike his ire as he longs for days they'd play
the national anthem just before test patterns
screeched into the deepest parts of morning.
He could go on and on about **social media,**
**frosting-free Pop Tarts**, some past **president,**
**mainstream news,** and how he always seems to lose
interest long before they get to the weather.
And don't get him started on **turn-signal scofflaws**
and drivers who wait for arrows to turn yellow
before advancing, its sudden shift from green
just enough to draw attention from the phone
in their hands to the highway ahead.
Every nit seems a gnat strained at, though,
as he considers this furry companion at his side
and how when he was young, such dogs were left
chained outside for days through blazing heat
and bitter cold, but no one blinked an eye.

**My Pandemic Face**

In seasons of pandemic,
my beard grows
a face unfamiliar,
smiles once broad
breaking in the bramble.
With clipped lips,
short words turn
strangely snarled
by simple things:

kind greetings

days fleeting

and so much less
talk about the weather.

Cheeks flushed ruddy
by holiday cheer disappear
in the prickly present,
an uneven cover
of stubborn brown whiskers
mixed in with the gray,
no normal to be found
amid the razor's rust.

Soon I may sweep
away this salt-and-pepper
contour for clearer countenance.
But for now, blades stay
sheathed as we wait
for better days,
every calendar square
a countdown whispered,
every hour a gift ungiven
until we're whole once more.

**The New Normal**

Retreat is the only option
when home becomes unfamiliar
and long afternoons turn into long evenings
falling for Mary Tyler Moore and Mad Men,
their spells streaming into eager eyes so hungry
for friendship and conversations, even the one-sided kind
that sometimes are interrupted by an overtaxed internet that bows
beneath the weight of neighbors who also ride the silent spiders in search of answers
and questions and diversions and names of long-forgotten loves and first-grade teachers
and animals left off the ark, as well as George Soros conspiracies and Schoolhouse Rock
anthems sung by grunge stars and going theories on why the metric system failed
to take hold in the '70s, back when information was true and delivered nightly
by well-dressed newscasters with so much more

~~truth~~ (nay)
~~integrity~~ (nay)
~~gravity~~ (maybe)
~~reality~~ (nope)
~~hope~~ (or was that just me)
(then let's say) reverence

than all the funny themes and memes
and their distorted photos of distorted quotes
of distorted politicians and funny felines
practicing their irony on weepy and deserving victims.

And when sleep comes with its promise
of something beyond darkness, it finds us
willing and lead-headed volunteers
stumbling through dreamscapes molded
by algorithms and artists of public relations
from Bangkok to Boston to Beijing
with no more malice than targeted ads
and all the truth 144 characters can contain.

**The Closest I'll Ever Come to Knowing (What It's Like to Drive while Black)**

Each day on the way home from school,
my best friend and I would bike past a yard
where that retired K-9 snarled and barked
from behind a chain metal fence.
We'd slow down and avert our gaze
as it eyed our advance, a red-and-white
**BEWARE OF DOG** sign unneeded but heeded.
One afternoon, the gate stood open wide
as the German Shepherd charged
from beyond a well-kept hedge.

I dropped my bike and froze
against the base of an oak;
my friend pedaled as fast as he could
but was unable to escape the angry dog's chase,
its teeth bloodying his heels and calves.
For minutes that felt like days, I stayed
motionless against that tree, its thick grooves
pinching hard against my back before the beast
finally lost interest amid my inertness.

Everyone I told said I did it right,
but fifty years later I can still feel
the beast's warm breath against my pant leg,
the menace of his growl as blood raced
until I was about to faint,
sweat mingling with tears
streaked across flushed cheeks.

**Get Small**

The senator says when bullets fly
I should try my very best to *get small,*
so I do.
I pull knees my knees to my chest
and then rest my head on them to pray
God's plan is kind, just, and merciful
this time
while headline news breaks
my heart again and again and again.
TV scrolls and online trolls
shred every last ounce of sanity,
compassion reduced to debating
rifles, school doors, and rights
while we wither together
one child,
        one sister,
                one brother,
                      one friend,
                            one neighbor
at a time.
Every day the dead disappear a little
more than the day before, just like me,
shrinking shot after shot until all that remains
is calloused skin, heart, and bones wrapped
in an echo of hope forever falling
across tired and ringing ears.
How did this become so hard to understand?

## An Open Letter to Old Ben Kenobi

When I was young, Alec Guinness
said it best as he clutched his chest
and staggered about the Millennium
Falcon, grieving over the *millions*
*of voices crying out* into the void,
and then just silence.
There was no way as a boy
I could understand the master's words,
the disturbance he felt a kind of pain
not available to my 10-year-old soul
as I waited for worlds to unfurl
that were neither kind nor heroic.

But that was a long, long time ago
in a world that seems further away each day.

In morning I wait for updates
to spill through Twitter feeds
and Google alerts, a sudden cry
ringing from nearby mosque,
a lone voice pleading with me
to lay down the phone and pray.
So as missiles whistle over
Palestine and video offers war
in live time, I search for answers
amid the ruins and realize
this is of our own creation,
a battle of the virtuous and virtual.

There's little righteous in always being right;
there's so much more than simply settling scores;
there's not enough time to fall in line behind
politicians and pundits who proclaim victory
over foes and the ill-informed all while
so much suffering persists.
How do we find our way back to
days when hope seemed to spring eternal and
we knew the truth would set us free?

I want to return to that boy
who believed in a future not
bound by shifting borders.

Help me Obi-Wan, you're my only hope.

## Mitch McConnell Stares Out at the Sea

of TV cameras and bright white lights,
then offers the world a pregnant pause,
the first it's seen in years.

With glistening eyes, he peers past
the restless crowd of reporters,
past these moments deemed important,
historic, and critical for our nation's future,
and glimpses an abyss so grand
words cannot corral its majesty.

With lips pursed tight he shares a silence
truer than any talk-show wisdom
that rises in his break's wake.
What does he see there in the selah?
Where does he go when they turn out the lights?
Does he know? Does he care?

The senator turns his back to us all
and staggers somewhere we'll never see,
the glory of his gift forever lost to the mystic.

**Flight 370**

Tumult songs and angry seas,
I feel the pull of everything I've ever lost
when I look out over seething swells
of whitecaps and gray slopes.

Tinker toys
Dorm keys
Locker combinations
Gift receipts
My first marriage
Confidence
The moon on a cloudy night
$34.85 between car seat cushions
An iPad at the Amsterdam airport
Old friends' phone numbers
A little good humor
and a lot of my hair
70% of my hearing at that Ted Nugent concert
Too much laughter in the pandemic
The calm pulse of my grandfather's voice
Both parents;
first my mother,
then my father
and so many more,
and then the words
to explain all this.

I long to follow the waves
to see where they lead,
beyond the South Indian Ocean
where no one should ever go,
the place where mystery
becomes a dark truth
with no answers.

**See-Unsee-Sonder**

Outside the shelter on a Saturday night,
a man in faded jeans preaches peace,
pestilence, and the difference between
greed and need before taking a sip
and passing the bottle on.
The congregation calls for kindness
from those with places to go,
knowing this town offers a thin net,
only streetlights burning brighter
while dusk falls and the rhythmic sound
of creek water rises over the low hum
of mosquitoes, slow chill spreading
across the sacred grounds of the drowned.
Before dawn comes, they'll flee
for shadowy spaces between
past and present, haunted minutes
dragging for hours as they scour
bushes for somewhere safe to practice
invisibility, the promise of daylight
coaxing one last call before communion.

*A Mouthful of Moon*

**Funeral Songs**

Mother greets her siblings
on the steps of the church
where she married my father,
and my aunts married uncles,
and where, when I was young,
I took communion from a priest
who I thought was God, and if not,
someone who looked just like him.

But today there is no celebration;
they've come to bury my grandmother.
Or at least to say goodbye,
as fierce winter winds
have turned the supple Earth hard
and unfriendly at the cemetery gates.
The gravediggers, even with their backhoe,
cannot clear her passageway
into the great beyond.

Cousins, nieces, nephews, and neighbors
file into the foyer, seeking refuge
from the season's cruel breath,
their fingers dipping into the font
as they form a solitary line
for one last moment with Emily.
The room fills with whispers,
a song for the departed, the rekindling
of brotherhood a lyric for the long-lost
friends and distant family.

They come together and fall apart,
an improvised waltz with long rhythm
calling to the great-granddaughter.
Her curly locks unfurl as she spins
toward the center of the room,
tilts her head high, and throws back
her hands, this music lifting her to her toes.
A staticky sprite bouncing through the brood,
her smile softens the harsh air of morning.

But then, like a thunderclap on a cloudless day,
the air retracts with a caterwaul of grief
as the eldest throws herself away from the casket,
tears burning down reddened cheeks.
And the small girl scurries back to the safety
of the congregation, a forest of legs behind
which to hide until she finds the safety of mother,
gripping her with every last muscle of memory,
a return to reverence for us all.

**The Dead Don't Remember**

how hard it is to live,
smiling back at us through
photographs and memories,
forever beautiful,
young, content, happy,
with no sense of things
impossible or implausible,
only knowledge of the way
it will always be.
They speak ill of no one
and wait with great patience,
something we cannot do
even on our best days.
And then when it comes time
to count the cost of things
they've lost, they waste
no while in the wallow.
Even as their grip on our world
weakens with each successive season,
they seem to have the perfect life
if only they weren't the dead.

## The Glacier Warns Me What It's Like to Grow Old

Sunlight floods a telephoto lens
with blue skies, bears, and pine trees
flipped upside down and back around
as snow-soaked shoes struggle to find
fair footing this far from the park's main trail.
Eons ago where I stand would've been buried
beneath a terminal wall of jagged ice and rock
and everything else that couldn't escape
the advance of the floe as it clawed its way south.
But today, the camera captures the glacier
in retreat, a slow-motion contraction so slight
you might not believe it's happening at all.
I stand small in strong gravity,
its icy recalcitrance clinging to Earth
as it gives back everything it's ever been,
mountains and rivers rising behind in its wake.

**Smoke**

The thing they don't say before you die
is that after you're gone, you'll miss it all.

Summer days and the way
a sun grows just before it sets.

The sweet breath of love
goose-bumped across the nape of your neck.

Rainfall's staccato song
slapping across concrete outside your room.

The list goes on:
   the sting of soft drink/
   an infant's coo/
   hours spent alone with poems
      about stars and coffee black skies.

And of course, more time with family,
friends, and those you held most close.

What you never knew as true
is you'll miss the morass, too.

The angry waves of dread sunk
into sore shoulders, liver,
and face wrinkled by age,
you'll at last embrace
in these anxious moments
as they bleed into the gloaming.

Regrets about work, family, and lives
misspent once haunted perilous nights,
but no more, their collective pangs
like sweet milk to your bodiless soul.

As they return to you in the end,
those breakups, broken bones, rivalries,
lost friendships, and misguided deeds

become as a family of bees
nestled in your chest,

along with opportunities lost,
embarrassing words, and even the sickness
that drags you back into the Earth
as you scratch and claw for everything
that defined the fullness of life.

In those last moments, all becomes
as a swirl of smoke, the world's weight
slipping away while its shapeless essence lingers,
flickering in between the light and dark
and everything thereafter.

**Of Love and Rust**

Learn to love
the rust of frayed cartilage
and bones broken long ago.
Embrace their stiffness
the way that older men do,
and do not eschew the tides
of change or discordance.
Slow the world
from its maddening twirl
with warmth, joy, and charity,
and at last, make peace
with each and everything that fades,
every person who forsakes you,
every dream that is dashed.
Because from dust we are born
and through rust we'll return,
the nature of nature forever
testing our mettle.

## Forgive Me Lord for I Know Not What I Do

like at first communion when Father put forth
the wafer and I bit Christ's body in half,
the kneeling congregation agog in their pews
as the priest scowled down upon the sinner.

like the time Dad coached my team
in Little League, and eager to please,
I sprinted to third from first as fast
as stubby legs and heaving lungs could carry.

like when I wept into an open phone
receiver while interviewing the grieving
widower for an article, asking the man to spell
his wife's and daughter's full name.

like marrying so young the first time
someone I hardly knew and then setting
the luggage she left behind firmly
at the feet of my intrepid next.

Forgive me for friendships neglected,
birthdays forgotten, letters unwritten,
my fear of water stifling family vacations,
and far, far too much flatulence
over long road trips,
under the comforter at night,
and audibly among groups large and small.

Forgive me Lord for I know not what I do

in your name, prayers vacillating
between penitence and perjury, promises
falling like maple leaves across water
undisturbed by the busyness of worry.

in your image, the failures of my body
bound by slack muscle and torn cartilage,
its withering as certain as a change in season
filled with hope for just one more good day.\

in your heaven forever at hand, mercy
shaking me awake each time the invisible
hold out their hands in despair, rising and falling
back into a sea of sidewalk tents and cardboard.

Forgive me for never loving
my parents enough,
my wife enough,
my son and daughter enough,
childhood pets enough,
the mailman enough,
and even politicians enough
to show them all how much they matter.

Forgive me Lord for I know not what I do,
like every time I try to write something
true and meaningful and keep coming back
to tales of my dog, or daughter, or a desert
dressed in metaphor and simile.

**In the Morning, I Narrowly Escape
an Aneurysm while Putting on My Socks for the Day**

Each day, my feet slip farther away,
trembling fingers and dangling socks
tickling the tops of discolored toes.
Each day, I forget a little more
about what it's like to stretch into space
and not feel the curve of the Earth
as it runs the gauntlet of my spine.
Heavy breath fills the room as I stoop
to tug at frayed threads, face turning red.
I feel the ballast shift against my back
like an hour glass, each tiny grain
pushing me toward submission
as beads of sweat form across my brow.
If I can survive this growing old thing,
I can survive anything.

## The Shape of Morning

She says that tea soothes
her gravel throat, then sets
the kettle to boil as blue flames
rise through metal grates.

Like her, the tea is mostly water.

She smiles and listens
to slow gurgles as they churn
toward a seethe barely constrained
by the silvery slope of the pot.

This isn't what she expected:
the threat of persistent clouds
looming across every horizon,
each ensuing storm taking
a piece of her with it.
First her vigor,
then her hair,
sense of taste,
short-term memory,
and muscle tone,
each tiny loss
felt to her bones,
five years of fight
leading to this morning.

She grimaces a grin
as a low whistle rises
against the calm of sunrise,
streams of vapor escaping
into the kitchen air
between us, the sound of sudden
winds rushing through canopies
of trees, fall turning to winter.

**Father 1.0**

Father feared the mouse, its smooth white tail
a pale path to perdition, too much mystery
for someone who spent years mastering mathematics
and how to best yield pencil and paper to build
freeways in a world more concrete than binary.

Windows, cursers, key boards, and mail
all meant something else in his day,
no mix of electricity and languages of code
to keep him company on appointed rounds,
his only companion the lonely squawk of an old Motorola.

And as he left this world, he took it all with him:
checkbooks and pens,
a wallet ripe with cash,
baseball box scores printed in full,
and newspapers smudged with ink.
When they reduced him to ash,
no electric fans or paper airplanes
could be seen through the thick smoke,
no Polaroids, long-playing records,
nor manual transmissions,
not even the call of curfew whistles
wailing across indigo skies.

**I Wear My Dead Father's Socks**

They do not guide my steps like
his quiet and steady words,
but they comfort my feet.

They don't struggle
to stretch around the girth of
thickening calves and ankles,
leaving deep impressions
that fade only as I sleep.

And they are not weathered
nor weakened by gravity,
tearing with just a tug
as holes grow after
every step that's taken.

They're my socks now,
filling empty spaces
in a chaotic drawer,
pairs and orphans wedged tight
as if they know one day
they, too, will be lost in
between desert and sea,
or disappear into
the deep recesses
of a dimly lit laundry room.

**Watching ESPN after 2 a.m.**

I love to watch the old games
even when their glory becomes lost
to the analog song and bleached brightness
of old VCR tapes.
And though I still remember
the victors and the lost, I don't wish
for their final outcomes to change.
I hope for them to stay the same,
the same way we would over the years
argue for hours about a coach's call
or some small play that loomed
large in retrospect.
It's been too long since you rang
mid-game while we watched together
and proclaimed over land line
how this was the year

: that we might win it all;
: that we should just toss in the towel;
: that we'll have to go see them play.

Sometimes I watch the old games,
but they'll never be the same without you
here to explain how it meant so much.

## My Brilliant Tattoo

Grief has a season, the doctors say,
but I wear mine as a tattoo,
        brilliant and burning when new,
        swollen in the razor-sharp sting
        of its Technicolor freshness.
Even in lifting the gauze to share
its hazy shape with friends
and family, I am alien to myself
        in a form forever altered by
        the permanence of colored ink
        and lingering absence.
I feel the curve of its line redefine
paths where the hair was shaved away,
no strip of well-placed tape
or garment able to disguise
the image reversed in my mirror.

Through the years, this stain will
        quiet my tongue
        subdue my smile
        and slow my gait
through days made more difficult
without your soft, still voice,
fading but always with me
until I am nothing more
than memory and fine dust.

## Armageddon Didn't Come Today

Dawn broke
   birds cooed
      together we woke
         to the lightening sky.

We didn't ask why the day came.
We didn't try to affix blame.
We didn't let slip deep sighs.
while recounting our disappointment.

: We worked
: We paused
: We dreamt

The sun rose, and clouds formed,
shadows shrank, and then grew
back again.

I stripped back the wrinkled brown bark
from a Snickers bar and sucked the gooey
nectar from its shell, not thinking
how I'd go to hell if it weren't
prepared or ingested just the right way.

Buses stopped;
                buses started;
a whole universe of people worked,
and played, ate, slept, fought,
and made up, whistled, and coughed,
and thought very, very hard
about their so many things to do.

I sat for five minutes in the cool confines
of the Honda and waited for the song to end,
its slight saccharine resonance glazing
my eyes before I turned the key to leave.

The daily news oozed into the TV,
phones, and computers at work,
at home, and everywhere else I went,
its static spilling out like black rain.

I talked with my daughter about not much
at all, an electronic call from a moving car
somewhere on the other side of the world,
her familiar face enough to erase
the day's anxiety from my mind.

The sun set, the moon rose,
and I sank deeper into my easy chair,
far too far away from people and places
I hold most dear as hours slipped from my grasp.

All this and still Armageddon
didn't come today,
nor the day before;
should I hope for more?

### Menomonie, Wis.

Homemade ashtrays and macramé
are most of what I remember,
banana seats and baseball cards
filling pre-teen years with notions
the world would wait for my friends
and me to emerge into adolescence
unchecked by the hang-ups
our parents held so tightly.
We kept to ourselves,
said our prayers nightly,
and roamed the streets
looking for the next pickup game,
the same as older siblings had
but without a sense of allegiance
to anything but our latchkey gait
and a Bicentennial belief
we'd never make it to adulthood.

I drive interstate highways
along paths that once defined
alpha and omega, guided
by reflective green signs
and automated voice direction
from a half-functioning
Apple maps app.
*Go one block, and then turn right*
Siri says four times in a row
until we find ourselves at the start,
laughter breaking the tension
between my wife and me
while the kids sleep in the back.
No guideposts greet us
while we approach city limits,
twice passing the house that once was home,
the neighborhood no longer familiar
to straining and bespectacled eyes.

I want to walk up to the door,
to knock, to ask them if they know
any of the names of those who have stayed
with me all this time:

the Sweeneys,

the Radkes,

and Luke, the pastor's son.

I let the car idle and stare back
as if through thick mist,
no twist or revelation
no matter how long I wait.

**After the New Moon**

When the time comes, bury me
in the deepest part of memory,
the place where names fade
and last leaves lose their grip
to wild and icy winds.

When I'm gone, stop at the edge
of places we walked together
and listen hard for soft silences,
autumn days drained of sunlight,
and songs we once sang.

And when your days grow short,
I'll return to you in the fullness
of a harvest moon in October,
a pocked circle painted yellow
by chilled winds heavy with dust.

## Acknowledgments

**Dancing on the X**, *Nostalgia* (chapbook anthology) by Written Tales, 2023

**The Cosmos**, *Plainsongs* (magazine) by Corpus Callosum Press, 2022

**Out of Bounds Call**, *Pasque Petals* (magazine) by South Dakota State Poetry Society, 2022

**Meet Me Tonight beneath the Carnival Lights So We Can Say Goodbye to Summer**, P*asque Petals* (magazine) by South Dakota State Poetry Society, 2021 (originally published with the title of **Carnival Lights**)

**They Dance (Sundays at Nelly's)**, *Pasque Petals* (magazine) by South Dakota State Poetry Society, 2021

**Advanced Dungeons & Dragons & Deliverables**, *Pasque Petals* (magazine) by South Dakota State Poetry Society, 2021

**Accidental Kiss**, *Pasque Petals* (magazine) by South Dakota State Poetry Society, 2024

**Snow Day with Sophia**, *New Plains Review* (magazine) by New Plains Student Publishing, 2024

**Star Wars and Everything After**, *Hobo Camp Review* (online journal) at www.hobocampreview.com, 2022

**My Pandemic Face**, *Passagers* (journal) by Passager Books, 2022

**An Open Letter to Old Ben Kenobi**, *Pasque Petals* (magazine) by South Dakota State Poetry Society, 2023

**See-Unsee-Sonder**, *Pasque Petals* (magazine) by South Dakota State Poetry Society, 2023.

**Funeral Songs**, *Objects in the Mirror Are Closer Than They Appear* (chapbook), South Dakota State Poetry Society, 2021

**I Wear My Dead Father's Socks**, The Dew Drop (online digest), 2020 (originally published with the title Lost Socks)

**My Brilliant Tattoo**, *Loss (Lifespan Vol. 9)* (anthology), Pure Slush, 2024

**Menomonie, Wis.**, *Home (Lifespan Vol. 7)* (anthology), Pure Slush, 2023

**After the New Moon**, *Plum Tree Tavern Autumn Moon Festival 2022* (online anthology), (Plum Tree Tavern Autumn Moon Festival 2022 (pttautumnmoon22.blogspot.com), 2022

**Todd Williams** is a former South Dakota journalist who now works in the Middle East.

His poems have appeared in numerous journals, anthologies, and magazines both online and in print, and his chapbook, *Objects in the Mirror are Closer Than They Appear*, was the winner of the South Dakota State Poetry Society's annual chapbook contest in 2021.

Todd continues to work on several projects, chief among them a hybrid collection of prose, poetry, and prose poetry chronicling the first years of legalized gambling in Deadwood, S.D., (where he was raised) and the poker players, dealers, and others who made their home in the boomtown over the last decade of the 20th century. You can keep up with him and his work at www.deadwoodbears.net.

www.ingramcontent.com/pod-product-compliance
Lightning Source LLC
Chambersburg PA
CBHW030055170426
43197CB00010B/1537